Famous

Poisonings

Toxic Killers and

Poisoning Incidents

Phil Coleman

Table of Contents

Toxic Killers: Famous Poisoners and Poisoning Incidents

For decades, poison has been one of the most unique methods of murder in existence. Unlike the aggressive actions associated with shooting, stabbing or arson, poison is perhaps the only method of killing which can be delivered to an unwilling victim covertly.

When it comes to categorizing poisoning, it can be labeled as anything involving excessive amounts of toxic materials being pumped into the human body. Such toxic materials can be anything from arsenic – perhaps the most common poison agent, to morphine – a very well-known medical drug used to treat patients suffering terminal illnesses, and anything in-between. Pesticides, antidepressants, household cleaning products, alcohol, sedatives – these can all be categorized as types of poison.

In addition to these obvious toxic components, materials which are generally considered safe can become lethal when injected in extreme enough doses. Similarly, materials which are considered safe on the skin can turn fatal when coming into contact with a human's blood supply. For example, foreign objects such as coins, plastics, and pencils seem relatively harmless on the surface, but when injected into the bloodstream can turn cause deadly effects.

There is a clichéd image attached to the act of poisoning. When we hear the term poisoner, it often conjures up images of scorned Victorian housewives lacing their husband's dinner with an untraceable toxin, causing him to pass out only moments after ingestion. Of course, this is more Hollywood simplification than anything, as the reality of poisoning is usually much more extreme.

We tend to think of poison as something which only affects the victim's nervous system, however, this is a common misconception. Death by poison can be an excruciating way to die, often accompanied by internal burning sensations, physical searing of internal organs, and even physical symptoms on the skin.

The History of Poison

Over the centuries, poison has been one of the most common tools for taking the life of another person, whether it be through murder, execution or even suicide. The 'clean' nature of poisoning makes it a murder weapon for choice many people whose primary goal is just that – to end the life of another.

For example, those people who commit murder through the use of knives or blunt instruments often enjoy the thrill of carrying out the murder itself. With their actions comes sexual gratification, and in a lot of cases, death isn't the desired result, it is simply a symptom of their actions. Using a blade to carry out murder means that the perpetrator wants to hurt, whereas murder via poison means the perpetrator simply wants their victim dead with as little hassle as possible.

This, then, helps explain why the clichéd image of a poisoner is a wronged housewife targeting someone close to her. The common myth is that women will usually kill for revenge, convenience or financial gain rather than sexual fulfillment, making poison the ideal method of murder in all of these cases. We believe that women tend to avoid both the confrontational aspect as well as the mess left behind by more physical methods of murder.

In 1945, Sherlock Holmes himself said: "Poison is a woman's game", however, the history books tell us differently. Poison is mostly a gender-neutral weapon, with the majority of poisoners actually being men. However, it is much more important to focus on the psychological profile of a poisoner as a whole, rather than break it down by gender.

Poisoners are usually cold, calculated murderers. In all cases, their crimes must be planned out in advance in order to ascertain their effectiveness. This means they must procure the poison materials ahead of time, as well as make the necessary arrangements in order to administer the poison to their target. This is in stark contrast to impulsive, heat-of-the-moment crimes wherein nearby items can double as murder weapons.

This volume will delve into the extremes of poisoning cases, from a mass attack on the subways of Tokyo, Japan to cases of medical professionals playing god with their patients. Unfortunately, poison isn't just a woman's game after all.

Michael Swango: Angel of Death

Joseph Michael Swango is one of the most notable angels of death of all time. Swango was a respected medical professional turned serial killer, whose occupation as a doctor afforded him an endless supply of potential victims, as well as the perfect ruse to cover his tracks. Officials have stated that his death count may have been as high as 70 people, including the non-fatal poisonings of hundreds of others. Amongst his victims were several of his friends, a member of his family and even his wife.

Tacoma, Washington – 21st October 1954. Michael Swango was born to parents John Virgil and Muriel Swango. From an early age, Michael was considered to be a gifted youngster, showing much more potential in his academic studies than his two brothers. As Michael's father was a military official, his family were regularly on the move across America. When Michael was 14 years old, the family finally settled in Quincy, Illinois.

Michael Swango suffered a severe upbringing at the hands of his father. While his mother was a much more calming presence in the household, whenever John Virgin wasn't away serving in the military, Michael's home life mimicked that of a military training camp. His father was incredibly strict and didn't hesitate to administer physical discipline whenever he deemed necessary. John Virgil Swango was a feared presence in their household, not just by Michael and his brothers, but also by

John's wife. John was a frequent drunk, often using his intoxicated state to later justify his physical abuse.

Michael Swango was sent to a Christian school following his mother's fears that his academic skills would be too advanced for public schools. As predicted, Michael completed his studies with ease, eventually turning his attention to music and musical performance.

Michael accepted a music scholarship at Millikin University in Decatur, Illinois. It was here that, at the age of nineteen, Swango met his first girlfriend. However, their relationship would only last a few months before she ended it with him. Unable to cope with the emotional grief, Swango dropped out of Millikin University. It is around this time that those in contact with Swango reported his behavior to become slightly erratic. Swango then joined the Marines for a short period of time but decided against the military lifestyle. He received an honorable discharge in 1976.

Michael Swango then enrolled for a degree in biology and chemistry at Quincy College. It is here that his bizarre obsession with poisons began to form. He achieved his degree with a relative, given his academic mind, then set out to enroll in medical school. Swango eventually got himself a place at Southern Illinois University.

Right from the beginning, Swango's approach to medicine was deemed to be incredibly unprofessional. His peers reported him taking shortcuts during his work which many deemed unethical. He rarely interacted with his fellow students, choosing instead to spend his evenings alone in his dormitory.

As his studies progressed, so did Swango's one-on-one time with his patients. Some students began to report an increase in patient deaths following Swango's interactions with them. At first, many deemed them coincidences. This did nothing for Swango's reputation as an eccentric outcast, causing others to view him as not just erratic, but also incompetent in his approach to medicine.

Obsession

Even at a young age, Michael Swango had a curious obsession with murder. He was something of a war fanatic, immersing himself in the horror stories borne from the Nazi war camps. He found particular fascination with Josef Mengele – the Nazi physician responsible for increasingly bizarre, torturous experiments on the Nazi's war captives. He kept a scrapbook of images which he had clipped from newspapers and magazines – all of which depicted violence, bloodshed, and murder. By his time in medical school, he had amassed a collection of multiple scrapbooks.

Following his completion at Southern Illinois, Swango was then accepted to study neurosurgery at the University of Iowa

Hospitals and Clinics in Iowa City. His behavior here didn't change. He remained as eccentric as ever, often using lies in order to advance himself. At one point in his studies, one of his tutors witnessed Swango interact with a patient for only ten minutes before submitting an incredibly detailed report on her medical status – something which would be impossible given the amount of time he spent with her. This raised great suspicion amidst the ranks of the medical staff.

Swango failed his studies based on this event alone, however, Swango hired a lawyer in order to defend him. Not wanting to take the legal risk involved in expelling Swango, the university agreed to let him re-take the year.

Swango successfully completed his re-taken year, then in 1983, began an internship at

Ohio State. Again, students began to notice an increase in deaths following Swango's involvement with several patients. In addition, several medical personnel noticed Swango interacting with patients during times which weren't deemed appropriate.

When authorities investigated Swango's strange behavior, as well as the sudden increase in patient deaths, they found no malicious activity. Swango was then cleared of any wrongdoings. Following one year at Ohio Stage, Swango moved back to Quincy.

In the summer of 1984, Swango began working as an emergency medical technician for Adams County Ambulance Corp. In a similar way to his peers at medical school, many people found his behavior to be quite disturbing. He would regularly make his enthusiasm for violence and bloodshed known to his colleagues, sometimes telling them that he could "couldn't wait" to see particular injuries and incidents.

Only three months later, Swango would be arrested on suspicion of poisoning his colleagues. He had purchased doughnuts for his whole team, only for everyone who ate them to become violently sick. Following an investigation into the incident, traces of poison were found in all who consumed the doughnuts.

Police searched Swango's home, eventually finding countless supplies of drugs, poisons and all manner of poison-related devices. Swango's bookshelves were piled high with instruction books on how best to prepare and administer homemade poisons, and in

Swango's kitchen, around ten boxes of syringes were uncovered in a hidden compartment. Swango was then immediately arrested and sentenced to five years in jail.

An investigation into Swango's medical practice was then launched, given the suspicion that he may have been responsible for the sudden increase in deceased patients in the hospitals where he worked. While it was deemed possible that he had played a part in multiple patients' deaths, a lack of evidence prevented him from being charged.

Swango was released from prison in 1986 after serving only two years of his sentence. Following a string of unsuccessful jobs and a break-up with his girlfriend, Swango made the decision to change his name. By 1990, the name Michael Swango had become synonymous with death and suspicion, meaning no medical facility in the country would hire him. Therefore, he became David Jackson Adams.

Swango eventually found work at the University of South Dakota. He had lied about his work history and forged documents in order to convince university officials that he was a stable, competent medical practitioner. It was at South Dakota that Swango met his future girlfriend, Kristen Kinney.

Kristen Kinney was a nurse in the area, who, unfortunately for Swango, was already in a relationship when the pair met. However, this didn't stop Swango from pursuing her somewhat aggressively. Eventually, Kinney broke up with her partner in favor of Swango.

Kinney knew nothing of Swango's previous life until her friends began to theorize that David Jackson Adams may actually be the infamous Michael Swango. Unfortunately, Kinney refused to acknowledge these rumors, stating that her boyfriend was nothing like Michael Swango.

For a while, it seemed that Swango's bloodthirsty desires had been quenched. At his new position, he appeared to be well liked and respected by his peers. His eccentric behavior appears to have ceased, and never once made his fascination with death known to anyone. However, following Swango's application to the American

Medical Association (AMA), Swango's past then came back to haunt him.

The AMA uncovered that David Jackson Adams was actually the notorious Michael Swango. They then informed the University of South Dakota of Swango's past, including the suspicions of his involvement in the murder of multiple patients. The same day which the university became of Swango's true identity, an interview which a journalist had conducted with Swango while he was in prison was aired on television. There was no denying that it was the same man. Swango's secret was out. The university then asked him to resign from his position.

In addition, this was the first that Kinney knew of her boyfriend's real identity. She confronted Swango about his deceit, but he managed to convince Kinney to stay with him. He had told her that he had been wrongly convicted (which was the stance he had maintained throughout his imprisonment) and that he wasn't a dangerous person by any means.

Unfortunately, Swango's lies forced Kinney into a pit of depression. She began to suffer intense migraines which lasted days at a time. Her youthful appeal began to fall by the wayside. She lost interest in her work, her family, and her social life. For a short time, Kinney even admitted herself to a psychiatric hospital.

In 1993, Kinney left Swango and moved to Virginia. She began to show signs of improvement in her mental and physical health, however, Swango eventually convinced her to take him back. However, Swango was living in Ohio and Kinney in Virginia. The pair conversed mostly by phone each day, with their relationship showing signs of a renewed energy.

It then came to light that Swango had withdrawn all of Kinney's money from her bank account. Following the rekindling of their relationship, the pair had shared bank account details to make their financial situation slightly easier. However, this had simply been deception on Swango's part in order to find enough cash to keep him going while he was unemployed.

On July 15th, 1993, Kristen Kinney committed suicide.

Somehow, Swango manipulated the medical officials at the State University of New York into hiring him. Now, with Kinney out of his life, Swango's patients began to die under strange circumstances.

It would be Kristen Kinney's mother, Sharon Cooper, who saw that Swango was fired from his position as a medical professional.

Naturally, Cooper blamed Swango for the death of her daughter, and so was willing to go to extreme lengths in order to protect others from Swango's deceitful nature. Cooper sent letters to every possible medical institution in the country warning them of Swango's history.

Swango was quickly sacked from his position at the State University of New York, and thanks to Cooper's actions, was forced to undergo a necessary transformation. Swango went off the radar for almost a year, eventually being found under the name Jack Kirk where he was working for a wastewater plant in Atlanta, Georgia. The authorities immediately contacted the company, resulting in Swango's dismissal. It then came to light that all of Swango's documents which he had used to obtain the position had been forged.

Swango's crimes and constant reinvention had alerted the attention of the FBI. However, Swango seemingly disappeared following his dismissal from his job in Atlanta.

Resurface In Africa

It was in November 1994 that Swango managed to find himself a job in Zimbabwe.

He began working for the Lutheran Church following more forged documents. However, Swango's incompetence as a medical professional quickly came to light. His colleagues began noticing that he was unable to make good on his claims that he was an advanced neurosurgeon.

Swango's past seemed to relive itself once again, with many reports of patients dying whilst under his care. After several months of work in the Lutheran Church, Swango began to lose the enthusiasm had previously possessed when he first started. Other members of the medical team noted that Swango had become incredibly lazy, arrogant and unconcerned with the welfare of those he treated. One nurse reports seeing Swango leave the room of a patient in the early hours of the morning – a patient he hadn't even been assigned to care for. The following morning, the same patient was discovered dead in her room.

An even further case of history repeating itself, Zimbabwe officers obtained a warrant to search Swango's premises. Again, they found copious amounts of drugs, poisons and surgical equipment. In 1995, Swango was told to leave the Lutheran Church premises. Swango escaped to Zambia but was soon intercepted by authorities.

On the 27th June 1997, Swango was deported by Zambian police to New York. Following an intense investigation of his time working at various universities across America, Swango was eventually charged with three counts of murder, one count of assault, three counts of submitting false information, one count of defrauding, and one count of mail fraud. He had also been found guilty of two more murders in Zimbabwe, but legal restrictions prevented him from being tried for these in New York. Michael Swango was handed three life sentences.

Swango maintained his innocence but officially confessed to the murders in order to receive a less harsh sentence.

Aftermath

It came to light that Michael Swango varied his methods of poisoning depending on his victims. When poisoning his co-workers, which he reportedly did on at least four separate occasions, he injected a non-fatal amount of arsenic into their food or drinks.

Swango knew that killing multiple people at once would arouse suspicion, so he avoided this in favor of simply making them ill. Why he did this is somewhat unknown, as poisoning all of his co-workers at once would arouse suspicion regardless of severity.

When it came to his patients, Swango simply upped the dosage of their prescribed medication. Because he often treated patients who were suffering from serious illnesses, this gave him access to the most lethal medicines possible. In some cases, he also wrote prescriptions for drugs which he knew would interfere with the victim's recovery process, usually causing them further sickness or death.

Swango is currently serving his life sentences in ADX Florence in Fremont County, Colorado.

Richard Kuklinski: The Iceman

Carrying out murder through the use of poison agents requires the killer to become acquainted with their target. Richard Kuklinski, more famously known as the Iceman, was a master of feigning friendship in order to kill his victims.

Kuklinski was one of the most infamous assassins of all time. Over the course of his murderous career, he worked for several different crime families, allowing him to hone his killing skills to a somewhat expert level. Kuklinski's murders became increasingly creative and extreme, with him eventually making the claim that he had killed over two-hundred people in ways never heard of before.

Richard Kuklinski was born on 11th April 1935 in Jersey City, New Jersey. His upbringing consisted of a strict, daily regiment which involved preparing himself for his school day as well as helping his two younger brothers do the same. His parents, Anna and Stanley Kuklinski were somewhat absent from their children's lives for the majority of their childhood. Both Anna and Stanley were devoutly religious, and both regularly indulged in heavy drinking sessions. Richard, as well as his brothers, were often the victims of excessive physical abuse.

In a particular harrowing beating, Richard's younger brother Florian Kuklinski was beaten to death by their father. Anna and Stanley took Florian's lifeless body to the nearby hospital and claimed that he had fallen down the stairs. Richard, becoming aware of the severity of his parents' actions, fled his family home at the age of 16. By this time, Richard had already become known for his capacity for violence which had stemmed from his troubled home life.

The First Victim

During his childhood years, Richard Kuklinski was bullied by a child in the same year named Charley Lane. Lane was a leader of a local gang who regularly beat on Kuklinski whenever the opportunity arose. After a brutal beating at the hands of the gang, Kuklinski tracked down Lane when he was walking alone through an area near their school. Using a thick plank of wood which Kuklinski had found nearby, he blitz attacked Lane from behind. He then beat him to death and removed Lane's fingertips with a saw. Kuklinski dumped Lane's body in a river. To this day, the body of Charley Lane hasn't been found.

The news of Lane's death quickly spread, although Kuklinski's involvement would not be known for a while. Lane's gang became concerned for their own well-being, although this only spurred Kuklinski on further. One by one, Kuklinski beat each member of Lane's gang to death with a metal pipe. This would just be the beginning of his reign of terror.

Crime Family Involvement

During his late teens, Kuklinski became acquainted with the Gambino crime family. He was picked up by famous gangster Roy DeMeo who hired Kuklinski to perform small time robberies for him. However, when DeMeo realized that Kuklinski had a real talent for murder, he decided to put Kuklinski's skills to the test.

DeMeo took Richard Kuklinski for a drive around the streets of New Jersey. DeMeo parked his car on a city side street and pointed to a man walking his dog. DeMeo ordered Kuklinski to kill him.

With no hesitation whatsoever, Kuklinski exited the car, pulled out a gun and shot the man in the head. He then returned to the car and the pair fled. From that moment, Richard Kuklinski became DeMeo's most respected hitman.

For over thirty years, Kuklinski claimed that he killed around two-hundred people, either by use of knife, gun, strangulation or his favorite method of murder: poison. While the exact number of his victims have never been ascertained, authorities believe it to be somewhere around the thirty mark.

Kuklinski most preferred type of poison to use to dispatch his victims was cyanide. Cyanide incapacitated the body quickly and was difficult for coroners to detect in an autopsy. The effects it caused also mimicked other natural causes of death, and it was generally considered to be an easy way to commit suicide. Therefore, this could send investigating officers down a wrong track when looking for the cause of death.

To administer the cyanide, Kuklinski would either apply it to the victim's skin in liquid form, via an aerosol spray, injection or by putting into their food. Once his target was incapacitated, he would restrain them and wait for death to take hold. He would then dispose of their bodies either in a river, in a shallow grave in the woods or by placing it in an oil drum to decompose. On two occasions, he also claims to have left bodies hidden in vehicles which he then sent for demolition.

Another Life

During his time as an assassin, Kuklinski met Barbara Pedrici, his future wife. The pair would go on to have three children together – two daughters and a son. Throughout their entire time together, neither Kuklinski's wife nor children were aware of what he did for a living. He simply told them he was a businessman, although he never divulged any specific details.

The original nickname given to Kuklinski by DeMeo was "The Polack" because of his Polish heritage, however, this would later change to the "The Iceman".

Kuklinski became aware that he could throw investigators off his tracks by manipulating the time of his victim's deaths. Kuklinski used a giant industrial freezer to keep his victims frozen for a certain length of time before disposing of them. Kuklinski believed that when an autopsy was performed on such a body, their time of death would be different than the reality, by at which point, Kuklinski would have an alibi for his whereabouts.

Kuklinski claimed that he would occasionally use an ice cream truck to freeze his bodies, although this was never officially verified. He later told police that he based the idea on a local hitman known as "Mister Softee" who drove a Mister Softee truck as a ruse. The hitman, whose real name was Robert Pronge, was reportedly an ex-military bomb expert. Pronge is the man who Kuklinski claims taught him to administer cyanide in increasingly elaborate ways.

Pronge would later be found dead inside his Mister Softee truck, with many people believing Kuklinski to be the killer. The exact reasons why remain unknown.

Kuklinski's trick was discovered when police found a body in a shallow grave which had fragments of ice still inside its body.

Capture

It was in 1986 that authorities finally became aware of the horrors carried out by Richard Kuklinski. Kuklinski had successfully managed to slip by the radar of the police thanks to his expertise in poisoning techniques, as well as the DeMeo crime family helping him to cover his traces. Unfortunately for Kuklinski, an undercover officer for the New Jersey State Police had become acquainted with Kuklinski, and Kuklinski had accidentally let slip a few crucial details.

In order to trap Kuklinski, the officer had acted as though he wanted to hire Kuklinski to carry out a contract killing. Kuklinski then revealed the exact details of how he would execute it, and his method of murder was consistent with some of the bodies police had already uncovered. Soon, authorities bordered off Kuklinski's street where he lived. It reportedly took almost 5 police officers to physically subdue him.

Imprisonment and Death

In 1988, Kuklinski was convicted of five murders, resulting in five life sentences.

Fifteen years later, he also confessed to murdering a New York police officer with a shotgun. This added another thirty years to his sentence. By the time Kuklinski was eligible for parole, he would be 160 years old.

During his time in prison, Kuklinski confessed to an almost unbelievable amount of killings, however, many experts believe that Kuklinski is embellishing the truth somewhat. He most certainly committed more than the five murders he was convicted of, but the reality is somewhere between the five and thirty marks.

Additionally, Kuklinski claimed that the severity of torture involved in his murders escalated exponentially over his thirty-year career. Aside from poison and guns, he also stated that he killed victims through the use of crossbows, fire and simply restraining them and leaving them to die of dehydration.

In two particularly extreme cases, Kuklinski reported that his client requested their target to be murdered in the cruelest way imaginable. Not one to back down from a challenge, Kuklinski stated that he bound a man to a chair then fed him alive to rats. Kuklinski further claimed that he filmed the entire ordeal for his client in order to prove that the victim suffered.

In another case, Kuklinski's target was a particularly religious man. When Kuklinski held a gun to his head, the man began to pray to God to save him. Kuklinski told the man that he would give him thirty minutes, and if God didn't save him in that time, he would execute him. Thirty minutes later, Kuklinski shot him in the back of the head.

On 5th March 2006, Richard Kuklinski passed away in bed at Francis Medical Center in Trenton, New Jersey. He was 70 years old.

In an ironic ending to Kuklinski's story, it came to light that for his final few years, Kuklinski believed that the Gambino family he had worked for were trying to poison him whilst he was in prison. The day following Kuklinski's death, he had been scheduled to testify against his former boss who had been suspected of organizing a hit on an NYPD officer. While the official ruling states that he died of natural causes, the mystery surrounding his final days is certainly a fitting conclusion to the tale of Richard Kuklinski.

The Tokyo Subway Attacks

On 22nd March 1995, a group of cultists released large amounts of nerve gas into the subways of Tokyo, Japan. The attack, orchestrated by the Aum Shinrokyo cult, was responsible for the deaths of twelve people, as well as injuring over 6000 others. The incident has come to be known as the Tokyo Subway Attacks, or the Tokyo Sarin Incident.

It was a rush hour Monday morning like any other. The Tokyo subway was packed with commuters, tourists, businessmen, and travelers. Amongst these people were the five perpetrators who had offered their expert services in order to carry out a poisoning on a grand scale: Iku Hayashi,

Kenichi Hirose, Toru Toyoda, Masato Yokoyama, and Yasuo Hayashi.

All of these men were members of a religious cult known as Aum Shinrokyo, headed by the enigmatic figure Shoko Asahara. Shoko Asahara was something of an eccentric; he was known across Japan as a mysterious, spiritual figure who referred to himself as the second coming of Christ. In addition to his radical ideas, he prophesied that an oncoming World War Three would lead do a worldwide Armageddon, resulting in the complete destruction of everything and everyone on the planet.

The History of Aum Shinrokyo

The Aum Shinrokyo cult allegedly had long-standing connections with North Korean and

Russian military, as well as connections with the yakuza (the Japanese equivalent of the mafia). According to reports, cult members received training from Russian and North Korean forces in how to create sarin from raw ingredients found in the natural world. In addition to poisons, cult members also trained extensively in the use of weapons and hand-to-hand combat.

Three years before the sarin attacks, Aum Shinrokyo reportedly purchased a large weapons facility in a bordered-off area of Japan. The cult's leader was also in talks of purchasing tanks as well as other military-grade machinery and weaponry. Fortunately, the cult was taken down before these plans came to fruition.

The Attack

Purposely situated at different parts of the railroad, each cult member carried with them a plastic or aluminum container loaded with sarin – a lethal chemical agent considered to be a weapon of mass destruction. It was placed in containers resembling soft drink cans and school lunchboxes in order to avoid suspicion.

Sarin was originally invented by German forces during World War II. The Nazis originally tested it their war prisoners but never used it on a mass scale. Originally, sarin was fired in artillery shells, meaning that if the bullet wound didn't kill the enemy, the effects of the sarin would. The chemical was designed to block transmissions between the nervous system, causing the chest to tighten and the subject to stop breathing. In addition, it can cause convulsions, burning sensations on the skin and an entire loss of vision.

The sarin containers were placed at certain locations aboard subway trains, usually in concealed areas beneath subway chairs. The cult members then pierced these containers with sharpened umbrellas in order to avoid being near the sarin when it leaked out. The cult had chosen its five particular destinations for a reason: all of the trains were headed to the same location at the same time: Kasumigaseki station. The cult's plan was for the five containers of sarin to all arrive at Kasumigaseki sometime before 8:15 am. The combined fumes would then equal greater consequences.

Cult leader Shoko Asahara made the decision to use sarin in liquid form (as opposed to gas form) due to its uniquely volatile nature. Even the tiniest drop of sarin on a person's skin is enough to kill them within minutes and is even more deadly when its fumes are ingested. Sarin evaporates quicker than most other liquids on earth, meaning that it can very quickly turn from a poison liquid into a poison gas. Therefore, people who weren't even near the liquid when it leaked could be affected by it.

Shoko Asahara had the idea to mix the sarin with the liquid used in perfumes. As sarin was entirely odorless, it was possible to make the poison smell as pleasant as they wanted. The cult reportedly mixed the sarin with sweet-smelling liquid to give a 'flowery' odor. Fortunately, however, the ingredients they used served to dilute the strength of the toxin down, thusly saving thousands of lives in the process.

Within a few minutes of depositing the sarin, thousands of men and women were said to have collapsed where they were standing. It quickly became apparent to those aboard the infected subway trains that something was very wrong. Reports at the time stated that subway carts and train stations along the Tokyo line began to resemble war zones. Bodies seemingly dropped to the floor without warning, some of which even rolled onto railroad tracks. Luckily, some people were less affected by the sarin than others, allowing them to step in to save any bodies which were in danger of being hit by subway trains.

All transport along the Tokyo Subway quickly ceased and all manner of emergency services were called in to assist. It became clear there had been a poison attack in the area, but the how and why remained unclear. Over the course of the morning, around 700 patients were transferred to nearby medical facilities via ambulance, and another 6000 made their way to hospitals by other means.

Amongst the symptoms of those infected were: unconsciousness, nausea, chronic stomach pain, extreme vomiting, loss of vision, breathing difficulties, internal and external burning sensations, dizziness, bleeding from various orifices, and mouth foaming. Eight people were poisoned fatally that same morning, which many people considered to be a lucky statistic given the severity of the attack. Over the following weeks, three more people would succumb to the poison's effect, taking the death toll to eleven. One of the victims remained in a coma for sixteen years, eventually passing away in 2011.

Aum Shinrokyo's motivation for the attack was to "set off massive confusion in the Tokyo area", according to Asahara. He believed that the police were intending on raiding the Aum Shinrokyo headquarters, prompting Asahara to divert the attention of the authorities. In addition, Aum Shinrokyo wanted to "purify" Japan in a cleansing reminiscent of the actions of God in the Old Testament.

Those cult members who carried out the attack were praised following their return to the cult's headquarters. Asahara lavished great spiritual fortune down on them, as well as gifting them with excess food and drink for the remainder of their days. Unfortunately, their free days would not last much longer.

Aftermath

Aum Shinrokyo's involvement was immediately suspected by the authorities, although some people believed that such a minor religious cult would not be able to procure such lethal quantities of nerve gas. Once Aum Shinrokyo's involvement was confirmed by Japanese police, they set out to capture the heads of the organization.

On 16th May 1995, authorities raided all Aum Shinrokyo camps across Japan. In total, there were 36 branches infiltrated by almost 3000 police officers. One hour before the raid took place, Shoko Asahara released a video to his followers with the message: "The time has come for you to help me. Let's die without any regrets."

Shoko Asahara was found hiding in a hidden room in the main headquarters near Mount Fuji and was immediately arrested. Following his capture, the extents of Aum Shinrokyo's crimes became apparent. Over the years, Shoko Asahara himself was found to have been responsible for the murder of at least eleven additional people (to the twelve which died as a result of the sarin attack). He had orchestrated multiple mail bomb attacks, several of which were aimed at high profile

Japanese politicians. He had ordered his followers to carry out several other poison attacks throughout Japan, and in one case, Asahara had stabbed a fellow cultist for refusal to follow his orders.

In addition to Asahara's confessions, Japanese police discovered stockpiles of chemical agents, class-A drugs, military weapons, around 7 million dollars in US currency, 20 liters of sarin, 30 pounds of gold and around fifty prisoners locked up in underground cages. Asahara, considered to be the mastermind behind the majority of Aum Shinrokyo's serious offenses, was put on trial. The following year, he was sentenced to death.

Following revelations of the cult's criminal offenses, Aum Shinrokyo was stripped of its designation as a religious legal entity. All of the cult members involved in the Tokyo sarin attack were captured and sentenced to death along with Asahara. As of 2017, the five main culprits, as well as Asahara, are still awaiting their execution dates.

Graham Young: An Unusual Boy

From a young age, Graham Young developed a strange fascination with poisons. While his school friends were dating and playing sports, Young was holed up in his bedroom devouring books on the subject of poisons and famous poisoning incidents. This would only be the beginning of a life of bizarre obsession.

On 7th September 1947, Graham Frederick Young was born to parents Fred and Bessie Young in the area of Neasden, North London. Bessie would die from pregnancy complications following the birth of her son, and so left Graham in the hands of his aunt and uncle.

Young's eccentric tendencies began from the moment he was born. As a child, he rarely said a word, choosing instead to play with toys and immerse himself in books. When he began school, he never socialized with any of the other children or spoke to the teachers. He was a lonely child by choice.

He remained this way until he hit his teenage years. When he was old enough to choose his own reading material, he immersed himself in true crime and crime fiction. He developed a particular fascination with Dr. Crippen – another infamous poisoner. This then led to an obsession with the Nazis and Hitler in particular.

Whenever the opportunity arose, Young would declare his allegiance to the Nazi regime – something which greatly upset and offended many people at the time. He even wore Nazi clothing and took to sewing a swastika into one of his jackets. As well as Nazi history, Young was an avid researcher into occult practices.

In school, his only enthusiasm was for subjects relating to science. He became academically advanced on chemistry, biology, and toxicology, much of which was a result of his extra-curricular studying of the subjects. At the age of 13, Young walked into a chemist and convinced a pharmacist to sell him incredible amounts of arsenic for research purposes. Young used his vast knowledge of toxicology to convince the pharmacist that he was much older than he appeared. Over the next few weeks, Young acquired even more deadly poisons, including antimony and thallium.

Only aged 13, Young was determined to test out his new wares. He eventually chose a fellow school friend, Christopher Williams, to be his first victim. When Williams' was unaware, Young laced Williams' drink with a combination of the poisons he had acquired. Very shortly, Williams began to suffer violent headaches and felt numbness all throughout his body. He began to vomit excessively – something which may have saved him from death.

Doctors were baffled as to how such materials could have found their way into Williams' bloodstream, as only medical professionals would have access to such drugs.

At this point, Young became even more infatuated with the idea of poisoning people.

He realized his knowledge of deadly toxins was incredibly powerful. He had almost taken someone's life and did so with relative ease. In addition, there were no signs of his involvement whatsoever.

He had wanted to study the after-effects of forcing someone to intake a cocktail of lethal chemicals, but he was unable to do so with Williams. It was then that he realized there was a group of people whom he could observe for a long period of time without suspicion: his own family.

Family Murders

Throughout 1961, members of Young's family showed signs of excessive poisoning on a regular basis. Initially, Young's father proposed that Young was somehow accidentally harming the family through the use of a chemistry set he had in his bedroom. He suggested that the toxic fumes emanating from the set somehow seeped through to the rest of house and caused a reaction in everyone other than Young. Although, on some occasions, Young did also fall ill along with his family members. Whether this was an accident on Young's part or whether he did it deliberately to avoid suspicion is unknown.

Young began to focus his attention solely on his stepmother Molly. He had never taken to his stepmother at any time during his life, perhaps out of love for his real mother. In November 1961, Young's father found Molly lying in the back garden in excruciating pain. She was clenching her stomach and violently throwing up. More sinister, however, was that Young simply watched her suffer as she rolled around the floor in agony.

Molly was rushed to hospital the same evening, eventually succumbing to her wounds. It would later become clear that Young had poisoned Molly with thallium.

Following Molly's death, Young turned his attention to his own father. Over the years, Fred Young became ill on regular occasions but never once suspected that his son would be deliberately poisoning him. It would eventually be one of Young's school teachers who would report his behavior to the police. In Young's school desk, the teacher had discovered materials relating to poisoning methods.

Young was admitted to a psychiatrist at the request of his school, where his endless know-how of poisons, famous poisoners and toxicology became known. He confessed to poisoning Christopher Williams, his father, and his sister, but didn't mention the murder of his stepmother. At the age of 15, Young was considered to be too dangerous to live a normal childhood. He was then admitted to Broadmoor mental hospital for a minimum of fifteen years. He would be the youngest patient in Broadmoor history.

Graham Young devoted the majority of his time in prison to study the art of poison even further. John Berridge, a fellow inmate in Broadmoor, suffered a fatal cyanide poisoning within months of Young being admitted to the mental hospital. Young eventually confessed to the murder, although how he acquired cyanide inside the prison walls remains a mystery. Young claims that he extracted the required ingredients from plants in Broadmoor yard, but how much truth to this is unknown.

In addition to Berridge's death, several other inmates' food and drink were found to be laced with homemade poisons, although he inflicted no other fatalities in his time there. On some occasions, Young's handiwork was also discovered on the possessions of the Broadmoor staff.

Throughout his final years, Young had managed to keep his poison obsession concealed from view of the prison officials. A handful of mental health professionals deemed Young to have been cured, possibly through natural maturity rather than through the assistance of a therapist. It was in February 1971 that a prison psychologist recommended Young's release back into the community.

Unsurprisingly, Young went straight back into his old habits following his release. Now at the age of 24, Young found residence in various hostels up and down the United Kingdom. His family had shunned him for his crimes, although his sister offered him assistance should he need it.

Within a few weeks of his release, Young claimed two victims – both residents at the same hostel he was staying in in London. Both unknowingly ingested thallium, causing one of his victims to become violently ill, and another to suffer such agony that he committed suicide. Young managed to flee the area before any suspicion of his involvement arose.

Young soon found work at a photographic laboratory in Hertfordshire. While his employers were aware that he was an ex-convict, his history as a lethal poisoner wasn't revealed to them. In July of 1971, Young's boss at the time, Bob Egle, began to suffer incredible bouts of sickness and nausea. Egle attributed to his symptoms to a bug which had been going around the laboratory (likely as a result of Young's more minor experiments), and therefore didn't seek medical assistance.

Egle had two weeks off work as a result, which allowed him to make a full recovery. However, upon Egle's return to work, his illness became even more severe than before.

On 7th July 1971, Bob Egle died at home whilst in excruciating pain. The cause of his death was ruled to be pneumonia, however, vast traces of thallium were discovered in his bloodstream.

Over the next few months, almost every employee at Graham Young's place of work fell ill with the exact same symptoms: cramps, nausea, and extreme vomiting. In some cases, employees reported hair loss and even impotence. Officials looked at multiple sources, to begin with: water contamination, radioactive waste, chemical leakage, but all routes led to a dead end.

However, when another employee – Fred Biggs – suffered the same fate as Bob Egle, investigators knew there was foul play at work. By this point, there had been over eighty cases of excessive sickness and two deaths. However, it would be Young's ego which would be his downfall.

An in-house doctor was brought in to the company so that he could provide emergency medical assistance should it be the case. When the doctor gathered all the employees together to inform them that the company's health and safety procedures were of utmost importance, Young questioned the doctor on why no one had considered the idea that thallium poisoning may be responsible for the constant employee sickness.

Indeed, the photographic laboratory did indeed use thallium as part of its operations, but it was Young's excessive knowledge which sparked the doctor's suspicions. The police were then alerted that Graham Young may know more than he was letting on.

Arrest & Trial

Very quickly, Young's history as a poisoner was uncovered by authorities. Following a search of Young's belongings, police found vast quantities of poisons and poison materials – including a hefty dose of thallium – along with diaries detailing every poisoning he'd carried out.

On 21st November 1971, Graham Young was arrested. He quickly admitted to his involvement of the murders of Bob Egle and Fred Biggs, along with a handful of others which the police weren't yet aware of.

On 19th June 1972, Graham Young was charged with two counts of murder, two counts of attempted murder and two counts of administering poison. He received four life sentences.

Throughout his trial, Young tried his hardest to appear as malevolent as possible, relishing the fact that he was now a famed murderer. The moniker "The Teacup Poisoner" was attributed to Young; a name which he allegedly hated. Reports state that Young had brainstormed media nicknames for himself in one of his scrapbooks, his most preferred one appearing to be "World Poisoner". However, Young wouldn't be so lucky to receive this title.

Young would spend the remainder of his days in Parkhurst prison on the Isle of

Wight, one of the highest security facilities in the United Kingdom. Within the confines of his new home, Young quickly became acquainted with the "Moors Murderer" Ian Brady. The two spent the majority of time together, bonding over their dislike of the human race and love of the Nazi regime.

Young's proudest moment would come following his incarceration. In the late eighties, a waxwork of him had been placed in London's Madame Tussaud's alongside a waxwork of Dr. Crippen – Graham Young's childhood idol.

Young lived a short life, eventually dying in his prison cell at the age of 42. Autopsy reports on Graham Young's body indicate that he died of heart failure, however, rumors still circulate today that Graham

Young poisoned himself as one last middle finger to the world.

Harold Shipman: The Poisoner Next Door

As is evident from the case of Michael Swango, the medical profession is not always as it seems. We naturally assume that we can place our utmost trust in our doctors, safe in the knowledge that they would never deliberately cause us harm. While it is incredibly rare for a medical professional to forego their professional duties in favor of more personal developments, there have been numerous cases of this assumed trust being abused by those doctors wishing to play God with their patients.

Harold Shipman - general practitioner, husband, father, and the world's most prolific serial killer - committed his crimes under the ruse of the trustworthy local doctor.

During his time as a doctor, Harold Shipman manufactured the perfect circumstances for a serial killer to operate under. He had a string of regular patients, all of which were elderly and suffering with various ailments. When an elderly person passed away, there was much less suspicion and investigation involved as it was not uncommon for people the ages of Shipman's patients to die from natural causes.

While some people don't consider Harold Shipman to fall under the category of poisoner, there is no other label which could be attributed to him. All of his victims were killed through an overdose of chemicals which caused their nervous system to fail.

Harold Frederick Shipman, born in 1946 to a working-class family, suffered through a troubled childhood. The overbearing presence of his mother, Vera, played a significant part in his upbringing. Due to the close relationship, he shared with his mother, his connections to children his own age suffered greatly. Any friends which he had would need to be vetted by his mother before he could play with them, and he never risked playing with the opposite sex for fear of his mother's reaction.

Despite his unhealthy bond with his mother, Shipman was highly successful in his studies. Not only was he academically gifted, but he also showed a great talent for sports. He became an accomplished athlete by the time he finished high school, showing great enthusiasm for athletics and football.

However, despite his good grades and athletic prowess, his social skills remained somewhat hindered.

Even by his teenage years, Harold Shipman's mother remained an overbearing presence in his life. She dictated who her son could and couldn't associate with both inside and outside of school. While this would lead many children to feel a sense of worthlessness and inferiority, it had the opposite effect on Shipman. Due to his academic and athletic success, he began to see himself as 'too good' for the other children at his school. This would be the beginning of Shipman's superiority complex setting in.

When Shipman was 16, he learned that his beloved mother was suffering from lung cancer. This naturally took its emotional and mental toll on the young Shipman who clearly idolized everything about Vera. Every single day after school, Shipman would return home and sit by his mother's bedside until she fell asleep. She suffered intense physical pain at the hands of her illness, only feeling relief from the high doses of morphine administered by the family doctor.

Eventually, Vera's cancer became terminal. In June 1963, when Harold Shipman was only 17 years of age, his mother passed away, leaving the young Shipman alone and heartbroken. He had lost the only thing he truly loved.

Shipman thrust himself into his studies as a way to forget about his troubles. He received more academic success following high school, eventually being accepted into Leeds University to study medicine. It was here that he met his future wife, Primrose May Oxtoby.

Shipman graduated from Leeds University without issue. He and Primrose soon moved in together, and by the mid-1970s, the pair had had four children together. At age 28, Shipman joined a medical practice in the Yorkshire area. His demeanor reportedly changed significantly around this time. Long gone was the shy, introverted young boy who attended high school dances with his sister, and in its place was an outgoing, aggressive and often rude young man who displayed behavior, not unlike those of a complete control freak.

In 1975, Shipman was caught forging prescriptions of pethidine, a painkiller similar to morphine, for his own use. The same year, he was fired from his position as a GP and sent to a drug rehabilitation center. Despite the lasting effects of this forgery on his record, Shipman was back working as a GP two years later in Hyde, Manchester. How quickly he was able to do this, given he was at this point widely-known as a fraudulent professional, is evidence of his ability to manipulate others into believing his innocence. It wasn't long before he was back to being the respected community doctor he once was.

Following Shipman's return to the medical field, suspicions began to arise regarding his professional conduct. Although he had a steady stream of regular patients, the mortality rate of them was much higher than any other comparable doctor in the area. While the majority of his patients were elderly women who were already in fragile states, the statistical probability of them dying at the rate they did was unlikely.

It would be a gentleman named Alan Massey who first began noticing a strange pattern regarding Harold Shipman's patients. Massey was an undertaker in the Hyde area who Shipman called on following patient's deaths, meaning Massey was one of the first people to witness the scene first-hand. In addition to the significant amount of deceased patients, Massey began to notice other strange aspects of Shipman's activity.

For example, Massey reported that many of Shipman's patients were found dead in almost identical positions. They would be perched on a lounge chair and leaned to their left-hand side. While this isn't an uncommon position for someone to pass away it, Massey became suspicious that all of the patients appeared to be dying comfortably. Massey commented that elderly people can sometimes fall out of their chairs or beds and end up laying on the floor during their dying moments. Similarly, Massey noticed that aside from Shipman, there was never anyone else present at the time of death.

He also noticed similarities in the positions the patients passed away in and the lack of medical paraphilia often located in the patient's house. For example, someone who required morphine would likely be suffering from a form of cancer, yet Massey noticed little else to suggest a person was suffering from such a condition. Massey confronted Shipman, however, Shipman denied all claims and even showed him his certificate book. After this, Massey backed down. It would later come to light that Shipman altered his patients recorded after their deaths.

It would be in 1998 that Shipman's actions would attract the attention of the authorities. One of his patients by the name of Kathleen Grundy – a wealthy ex-political figure – was reported to have died on her sofa under Shipman's care. However, it seemed incredibly unlikely for this to be the case considering Grundy's decent health. In this case, it was not Shipman who called in Grundy's death but her friends. When Grundy didn't show up for a weekly club which she was a member of, her friends went to her home to check on her.

Grundy's friends called Shipman to her home. When he arrived, he noted that he had been with Grundy only hours prior to her death under the pretense of delivering her regular medication. He also claimed that he had taken blood tests from Grundy for 'research purposes'.

Ship also told Kathleen's daughter, Angela Woodruff, that an autopsy would not be necessary due to him being with the victim not long before she passed away. Angela Woodruff's were suspicions were already high at this point, but the most bizarre incident of all came when her solicitor informed her that her mother had recently submitted her last will and testament. A will which excluded Angela entirely, and left the considerable sum of £386,000 to Doctor Shipman.

The will itself was particularly amateur. Not only was it hastily put-together, but Kathleen's signature didn't look genuine at all. Angela Woodruff also thought it bizarre that her mother would leave such a vast amount of money to a doctor she hardly knew. Kathleen Grundy was meticulous in her ways, nor was she short of friends, family or acquaintances. Additionally, the fact she passed away so suddenly raised a lot of questions, given that she was considered to be incredibly healthy for her age.

Unfortunately for him, Harold Shipman had clearly underestimated the competence of Kathleen Grundy and her family.

Angela presented this information to the police. They could now establish a financial motive in Shipman which gave them cause to investigate further. Shipman was taken into custody by Manchester police which authorities exhumed the bodies of any previous patients under Shipman's care. They also searched Shipman's home and his Hyde office, eventually uncovering several pieces of key evidence linking him to the deaths of several elderly women in the area.

In his office drawers were vast amounts of ladies' jewelry and other personal possessions. In his trash can, they also found medical records which Shipman had tried to destroy. However, most incriminating of all was the typewriter discovered in Shipman's office. The typeface was an exact match for the font on Kathleen Grundy's forged will.

Very quickly, toxicology reports from Kathleen Grundy's autopsy showed that the morphine levels inside her were much higher than her body could reasonably handle. A shocking discovery, given that they were administered by a well-respected medical professional and veteran doctor. When questioned, Shipman tried to tell authorities that Kathleen Grundy, a political figure and conservative lady in her 80s, was a drug addict. Of course, this was immediately dismissed as fabrication on Shipman's part.

After speaking to the families of the recently deceased patients under Shipman's care, it came to light that Shipman had 'advised' them to cremate their bodies and to not request any further investigation regarding their deaths. Something which, in hindsight to detectives, appears strange, however many people assumed it wasn't necessary to question the advice of a trained medical professional. Additionally, even if further investigation was demanded by families, all medical records had been altered to justify the doses of morphine Shipman was injecting. In the case of Kathleen Grundy, he would later change her records to match his claims that she was a morphine addict.

Despite Shipman's grandiose sense of superiority, one area he was not covertly skilled in was with computers. Although he claimed he was a "computer expert", it would be his falsifying of documents which would lead to the discovery of his previous victims. Shipman was unaware that every change he made to his patients' medical history was logged on his hard drive with specific details and time stamps. Police discovered that in the majority of cases, Shipman wrote that his patients' ailments were much more severe than they actually were, thus warranting an increase in morphine. Shipman was required to justify the amount of morphine required through his patient files. This was how he managed to acquire the vast quantities of the drug from his suppliers without raising suspicion.

When the police confronted him with this information, Shipman refused to co-operate and simply denied all claims. He said that he had never altered his patient's documents and disputed his claims that he was a 'computer expert'. In fact, he told police the opposite; that his skills with computers were amateur at best.

Shipman was taken to court on the charge of killing fifteen of his patients, and it was in the courtroom that his true motivations would come to light. It was said that Shipman repeatedly murdered because he enjoyed doing so. He emitted the ultimate power over his victims; the ability to control life and death. The court's first witness, Angela Woodruff, the daughter of Shipman's final victim, explained the inconsistencies between her mother's demeanor and Shipman's interpretation of her. The evidence was damning and there was no doubt of Shipman's guilt.

New revelations emerged during the trial. On many occasions, Shipman claims to have phoned an ambulance while his patients were close to death in an attempt to save them, yet phone records indicated that no such calls were ever made. The blood samples which Shipman claims to have taken from Kathleen Grundy on the day of her death did not exist, and there was even no such 'study' which he claimed the samples were required for. Shipman's stories changed drastically during his trial which only caused his credibility to wane further.

The cause of death in all of Shipman's known victims was an overdose of diamorphine. Defendants during his trial attempted to claim that Shipman did not carry morphine at any time during his home visits, but this was disproved by multiple pieces of evidence. Just how Shipman was able to amass so much of the drug also became clear during his trial. Shipman would prescribe hefty doses of the drug to patients in the days leading up to their deaths. Once he had administered enough to kill them, he would then steal the drug from his victims' homes and keep for use either on himself (it is believed that he was still an active drug user his whole life) or on other victims.

On 31st January 2000, Harold Shipman was found guilty of fifteen accounts of murder and one charge of forgery. His prison sentence was a total of fifteen life sentences plus four years. Harold Shipman was to spend the rest of his life in jail.

Shipman protested in his innocence all the way through his trial and has never confessed to anything. The reason why he killed is not truly understood. He is, by all accounts, a unique serial killer. The first noticeable difference between Shipman and other infamous murderers is that Shipman's crimes held no sexual fulfillment for him. There was no violence, no taunting, no toying with his victims prior to death.

Due to the nature of Shipman's crimes, it is difficult to ascertain his true victim count. Different reports have different exact figures, although the estimate is considered to be around 260. The world will never know the true number, as on 13th January 2004, Harold Shipman committed suicide in his cell at Wakefield Prison. He had shown no previous signs of suicidal tendencies so he was not considered to be at risk. Shipman's suicide perfectly embodies the deception he was capable of. It was a final insult to the families of his victims.

Shipman's wife and children have never been able to come to terms with his crimes, and it is understandable that they will struggle. A husband, father, and doctor who once took an oath to save lives remains the most prominent serial killer to have ever lived is a notion which would seem too farfetched even for fiction.

The Shizuoka Schoolgirl: Graham Young's Biggest Fan

Perhaps one of the most interesting poisoning cases – and certainly one of the most recent – deals with the subject of a 17-year-old schoolgirl from the Shizuoka region of Japan.

The girl, who remained anonymous due to her being a minor, poisoned her own mother and documented the happenings on her social media blog. The girl claims to have been obsessed with the Teacup Poisoner Graham Young. On her blog – two months before her she carried out her poisonings, she wrote:

"July 3: Let me introduce a book: Graham Young's diary on killing with poison. The autobiography of a man I respect. He murdered someone at the age of 14."

On August 18th, 2005, the girl reportedly dosed her mother's food with thallium – the same poison used by Graham Young. Within a few minutes, the girl's mother became violently sick, to which the girl made notes of her mother's ailments on her notepad. The following evening, the girl took to her online blog to tell the world of what she had done. Her blog entry stated:

"Aug 19: Mother has been sick since yesterday with a rash all over her body."

Two weeks previously, she had written:

"Aug 4: It's a bright, sunny day today, and I administered a delivery of acetic thallium. The man in the pharmacy didn't realize he had sold me such a powerful drug."

Over the next few weeks, the girl regularly dosed her mother with the thallium she had purchased from the chemist, continuing to document the effects on her blog. While her blog was seen by a number of people, it didn't immediately raise suspicion as it was considered to be fictional. Furthermore, the girl didn't explicitly state in the blog that it was her who was responsible.

On September 4th, 2005, the girl wrote the following:

"Sep 4: To kill a living creature. The moment of sticking a knife into something. The warmth of the blood. The little sigh. It is all a comfort to me."

Initially, it isn't difficult to brush this off as the ramblings of a fictional character, albeit one presented as real. Forums, blogs, and social media are rife with such outputs, therefore, the girl's blog was considered to be the same. However, the girl's next posts raised the suspicions of a handful of readers.

"Sep 12: She had been complaining her legs have been no good for two or three days and has finally become almost unable to move."

"Sep 26: My mother will go to the hospital tomorrow and nobody has yet found out what the cause is. To my regret, she is not covered by good insurance, so life will be a little difficult."

"Oct 11: I took a photo of her today as I did yesterday. My brother said I had a penetrating stare and that he was horrified."

"Oct 15: I got sympathy from my teacher when I tearfully talked about the mother. I guess people are cheated more easily than I expected."

"Oct 23: "According to my aunt, my mother has started having hallucinations. She seems to be suffering from insects that don't exist or white shadows by the door."

One reader reported the girl's actions to the local police, and upon investigation, the police found that there was indeed a woman in a Shizuoka hospital suffering from the symptoms described in the girl's blog. The police looked into the history of the girl's blog and found that she had been discussing poison experiments for the past three years. In her earlier blog posts, the girl reportedly poisoned animals and documented her findings. In addition, the girl was a member of a prestigious high school and she specialized in chemistry and biology – very similar to her hero Graham Young.

By this point, the girl's mother had fallen into a coma, meaning police were unable to extract any information from her. However, when police interviewed the doctors assigned to care for her, one of them informed the officers that the woman's son had mentioned that her sister may have been responsible for her mother's illness.

Police investigated the girl at her home in Shizuoka. They seized her computer and found that she was in fact the author of the blog in question. In the girl's bedroom, the police found all manner of strange materials: dismembered dolls, animal heads, bizarre drawings, various drugs and a stash of thallium.

The girl denied any involvement with her mother's ordeal, going as far to claim that she suffered from thallium poisoning herself. The girl's idol, Graham Young, reportedly suffered from thallium poisoning on multiple occasions himself, but whether or not it was done purposely remains unknown. The girl may have willingly ingested thallium in order to alleviate suspicion of her involvement.

The girl's mother died in the months following her poisoning. She remained in critical condition until passing away at an unknown date and time. The fate of the girl herself remains unknown due to the confidentiality around the case, however, it is believed that she now resides in a Japanese mental hospital.

Conclusion

As is evident from this volume, the motivations for murders via poison are not just limited to the clichéd scorned housewife extracting revenge.

It appears that poisoners' motivations for murder aren't much different from any other type of homicide. In the case of the Tokyo Subway Attacks, this was simply a way to incite terror on a mass scale through the use of chemical agents. While we tend to think of acts of terrorism as bombings, explosions or shootings, the actions of Aum Shinrokyo were as terror-inducing as any of Al-Qaeda's operations.

In the case of Michael Swango and Harold Shipman, the poisoner becomes a master of both life and death. Both were competent serial killers who avoided detection for a significant amount of time, and both used their medical knowledge and status in order to carry out their horrific actions. The fact that these two angels of death were as successful as they were in their murderous careers can likely be attributed to the fact they killed their victims through chemical overdoses. If Harold Shipman had used a blade to end his victims' lives, we can be certain that his activity would have been discovered much quicker.

In the case of Richard Kuklinski, we can see that while he was an expert in all manner of execution methods, poison became his method of choice. This is very revealing, especially considering Richard Kuklinski was a contract killer as well as someone who enjoyed the act of murder. This highlights the fact that poison may, in fact, be the most efficient method of murder possible. It can be delivered covertly, without the need for the killer to even be in the same room as the victim. It can be delivered in multiple different ways, and in some cases, it can even be undetectable. Furthermore, the act of poisoning allows the killer much more freedom in their modus operandi.

A particularly harrowing statistic is the fact that, as of 2017, one out of five poisoning cases goes unsolved. This means that for every Harold Shipman we catch, four more may be in operation. While we can draw some conclusions from the poisoners we do catch, it is difficult to paint a whole picture of a common poisoner due to the fact that so many go undetected. We know that poisoners tend to be organized, cunning, methodical, selfish and emotionally undeveloped, but there may be much for us to learn yet. One common characteristic which does seem constant across Michael Swango, Harold Shipman, Richard Kuklinski and Graham Young is that all of them acted under the guise of something they weren't: medical professionals, fathers, husbands, friends. Their ruses, combined with the transient nature of poisoning, made for deadly circumstances.

Printed in Great Britain
by Amazon

33864750R00065